I Am Ju

GW01237693

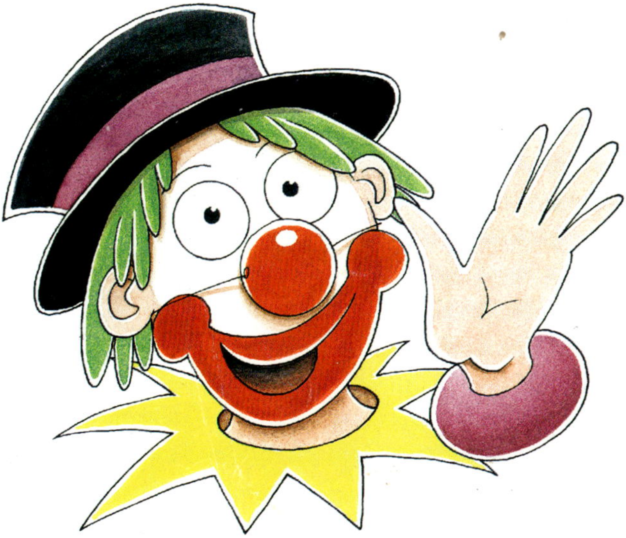

By Jill Eggleton and Jo Windsor

Illustrated by Clive Taylor

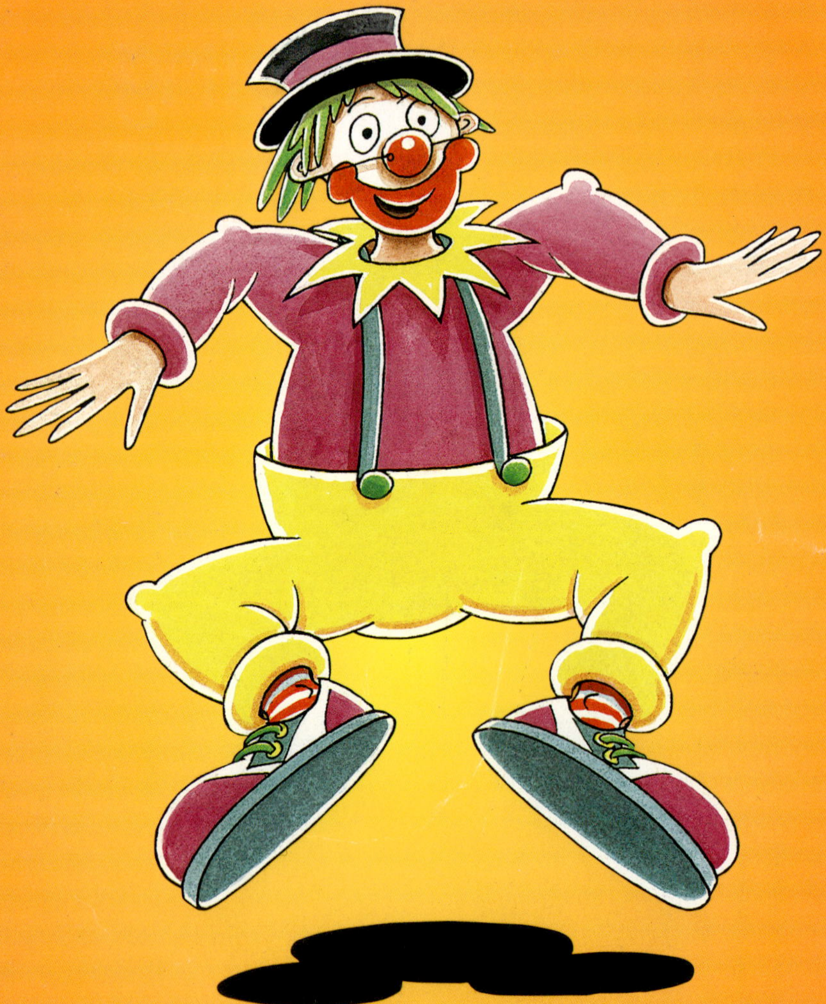

I am jumping.

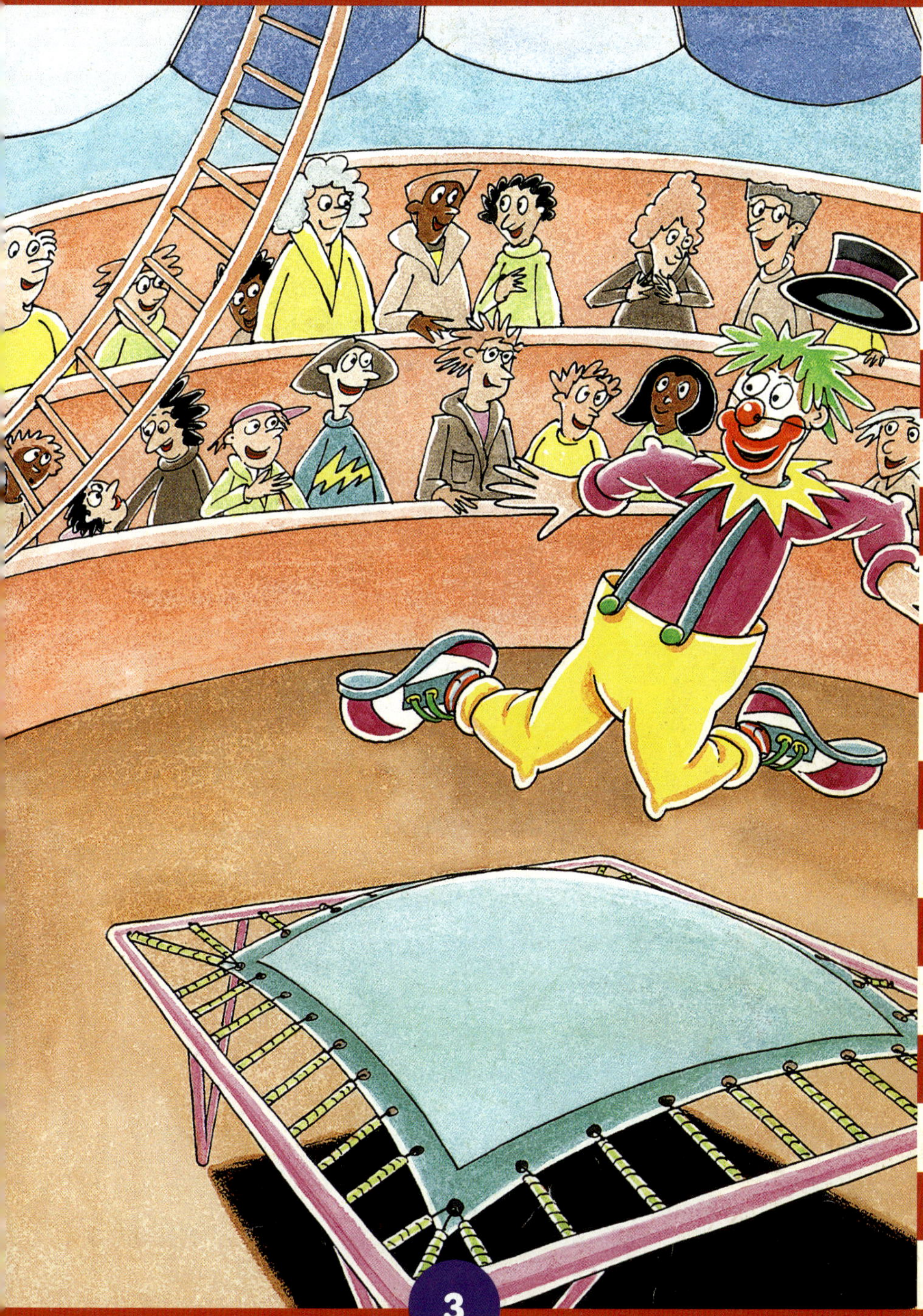

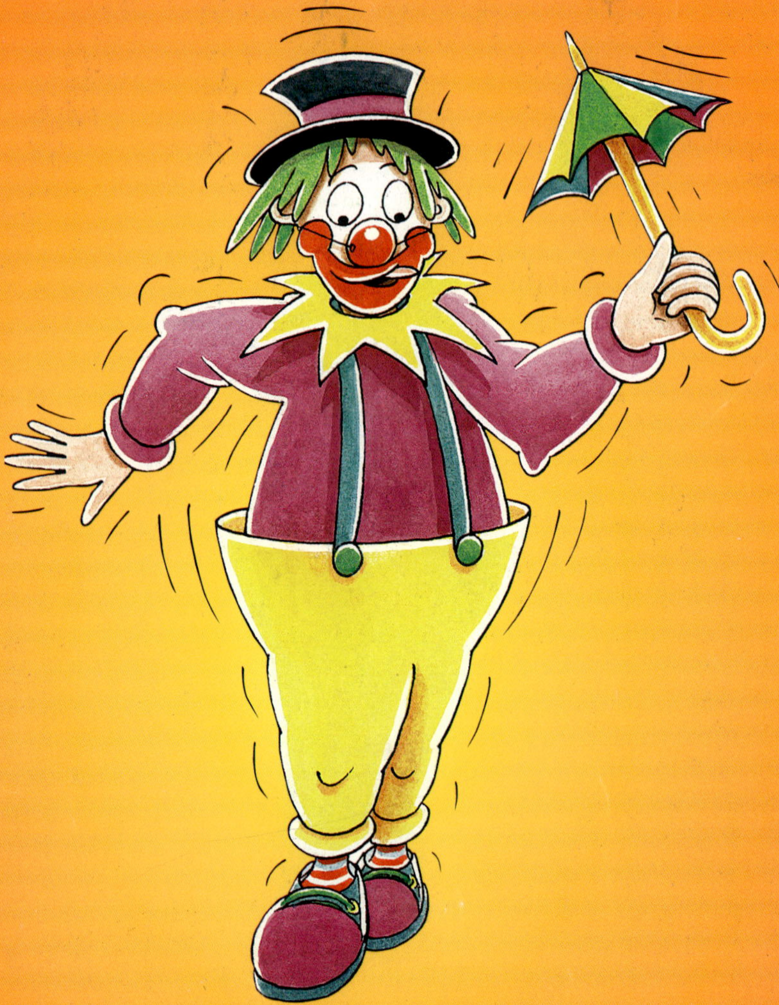

I am walking.

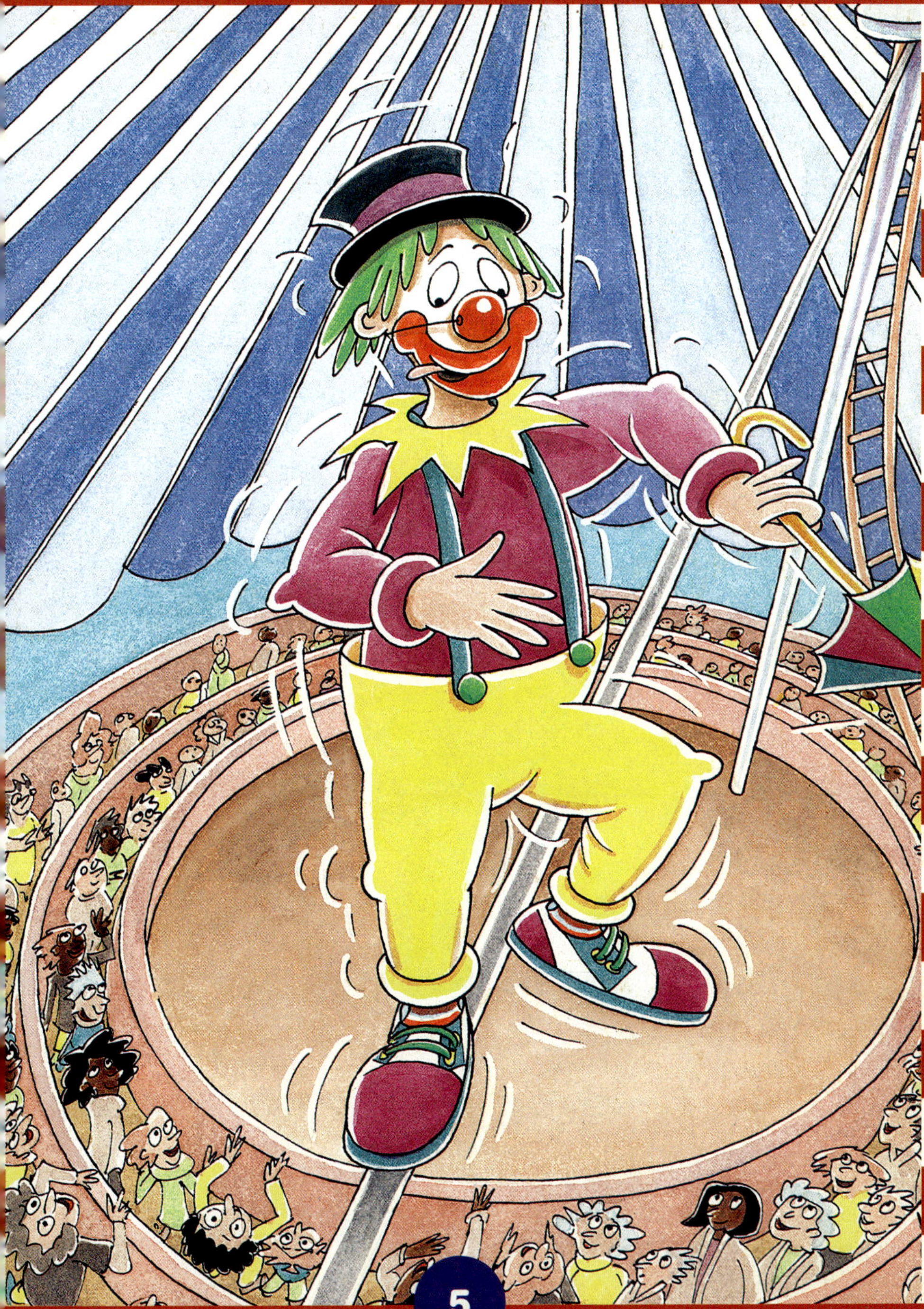

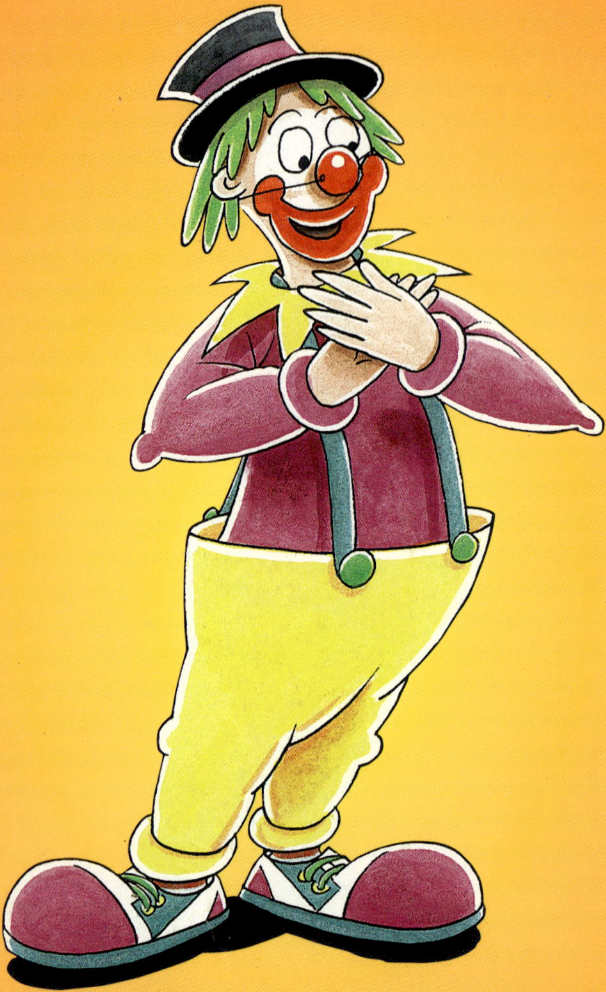

I am clapping.

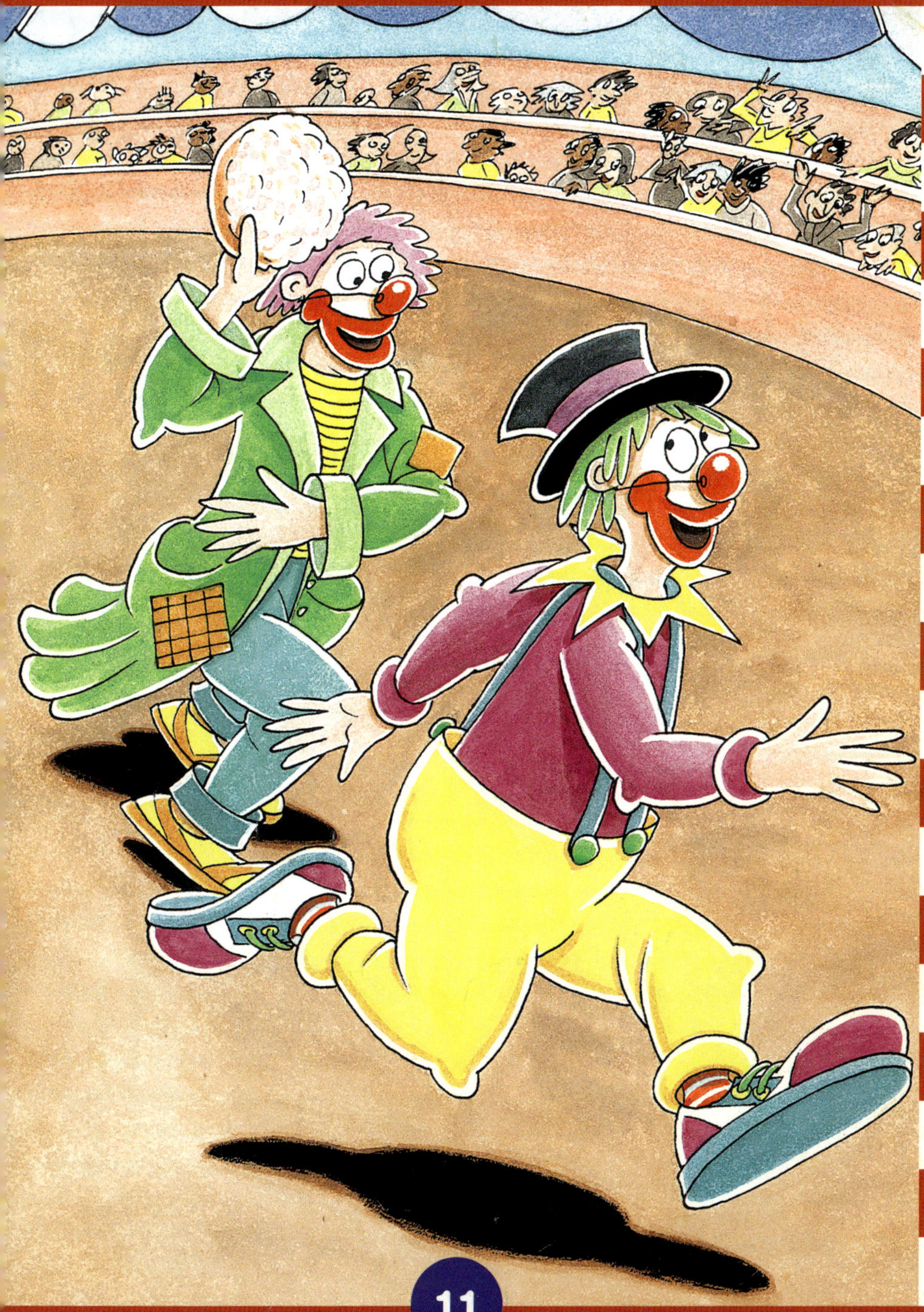

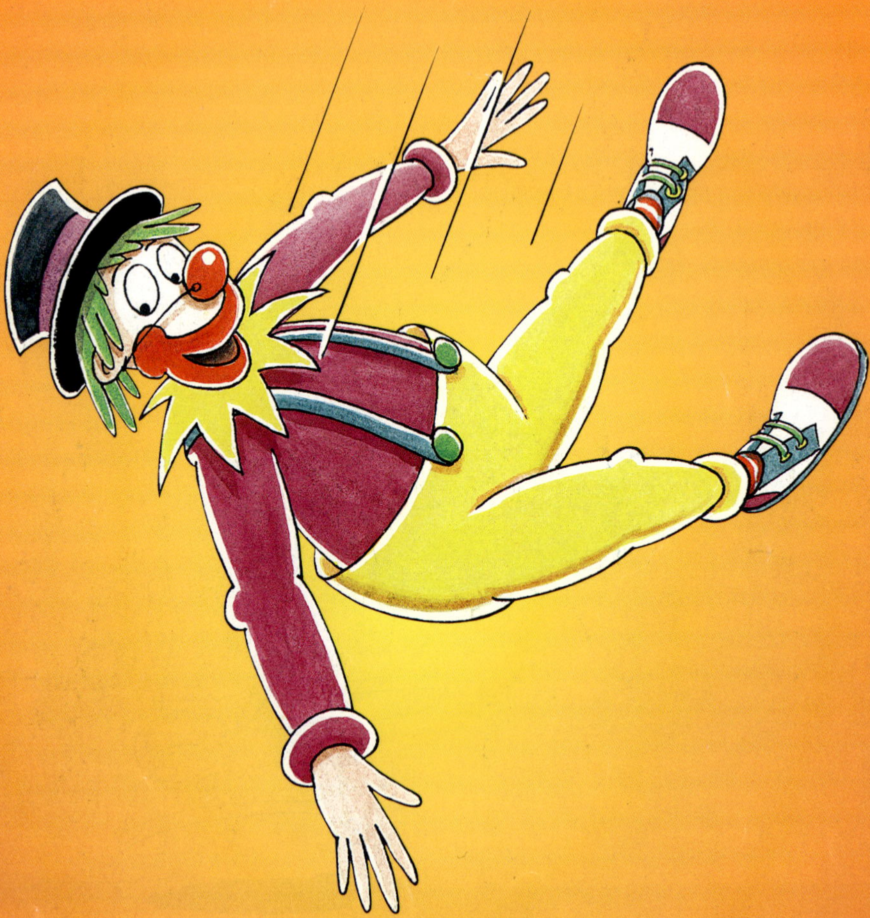

I am falling.

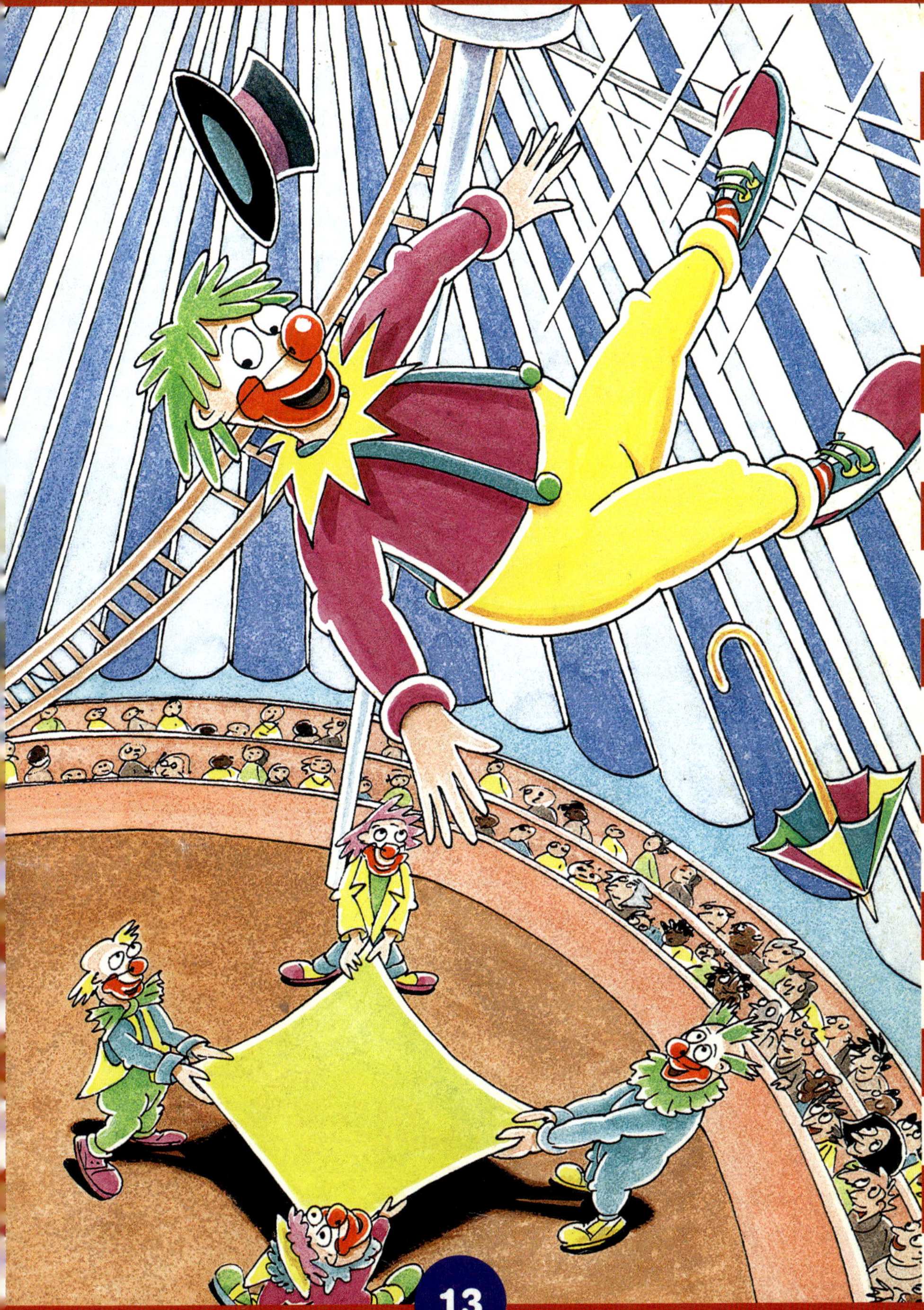

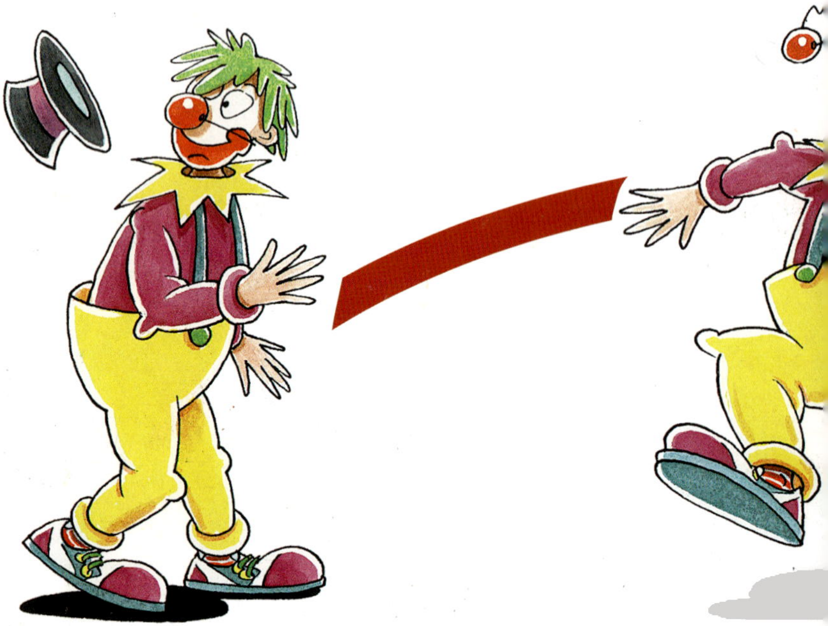

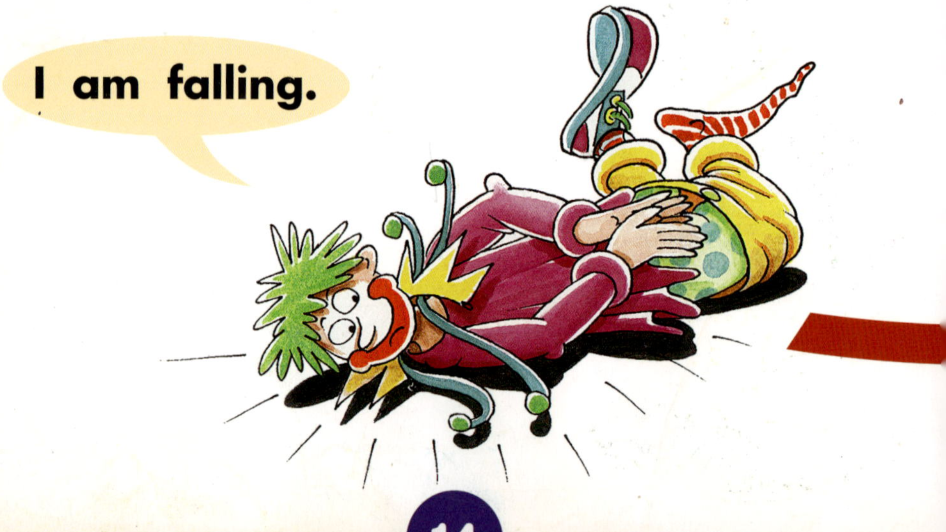
I am falling.

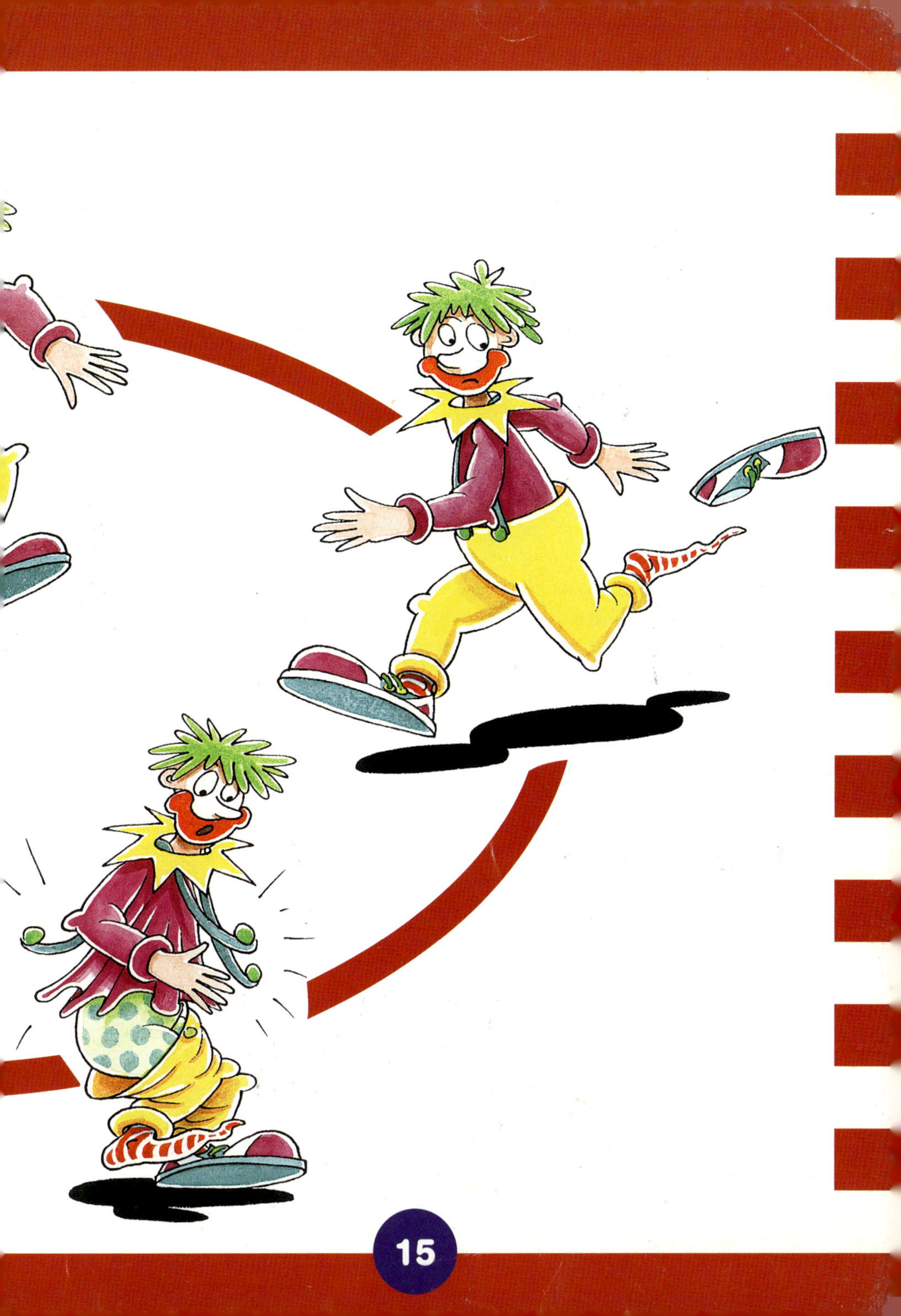

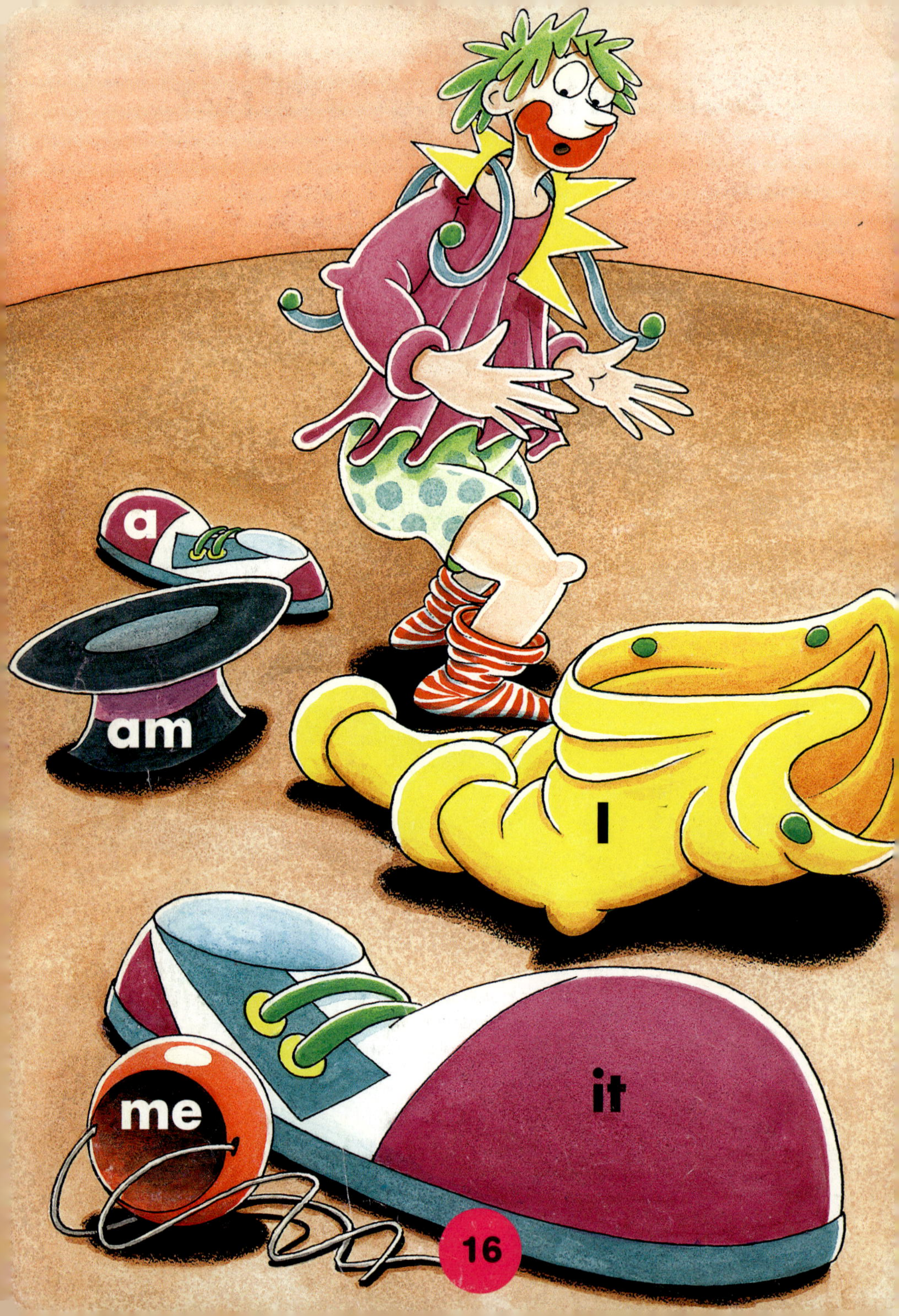
a
am
I
me
it

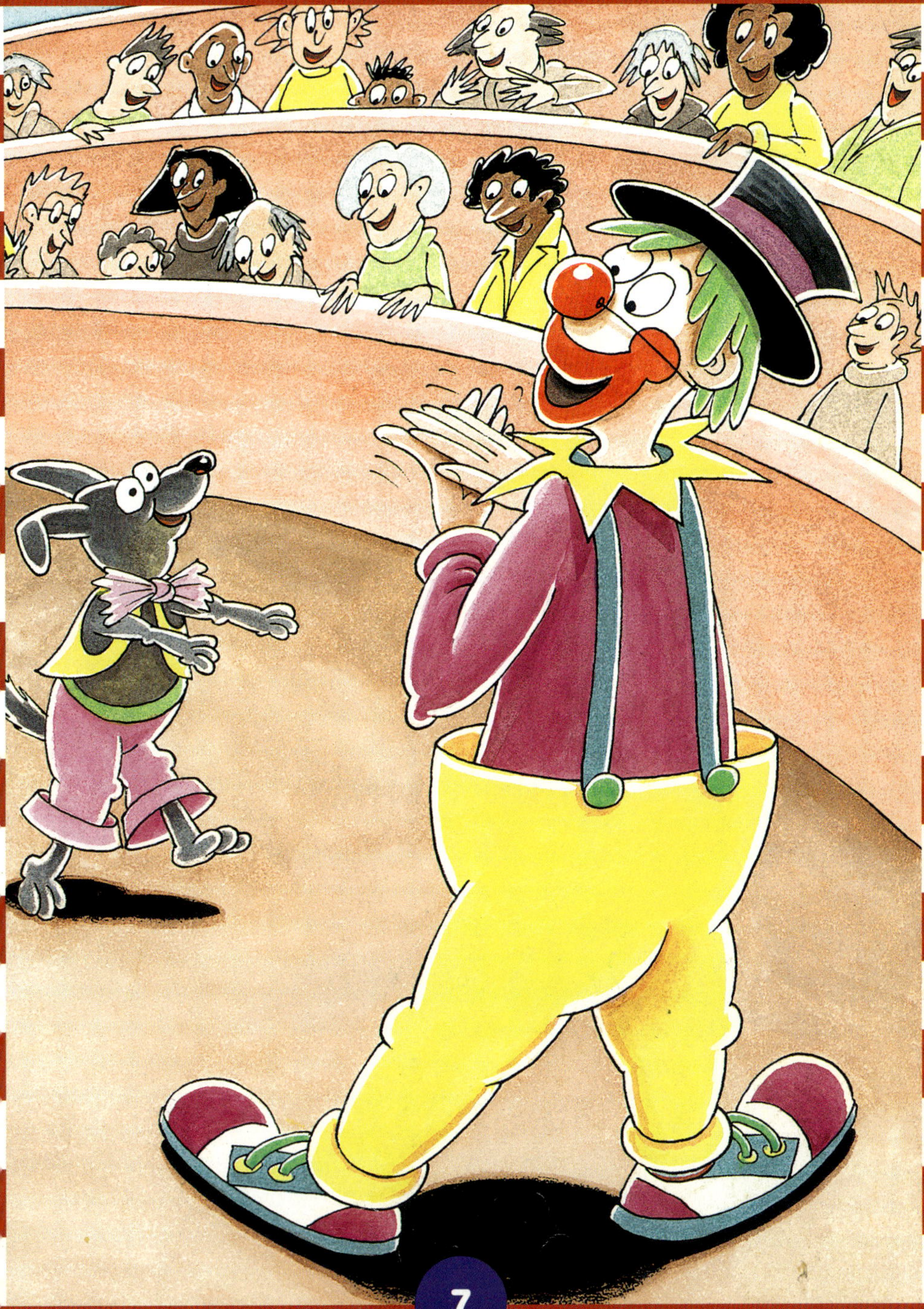

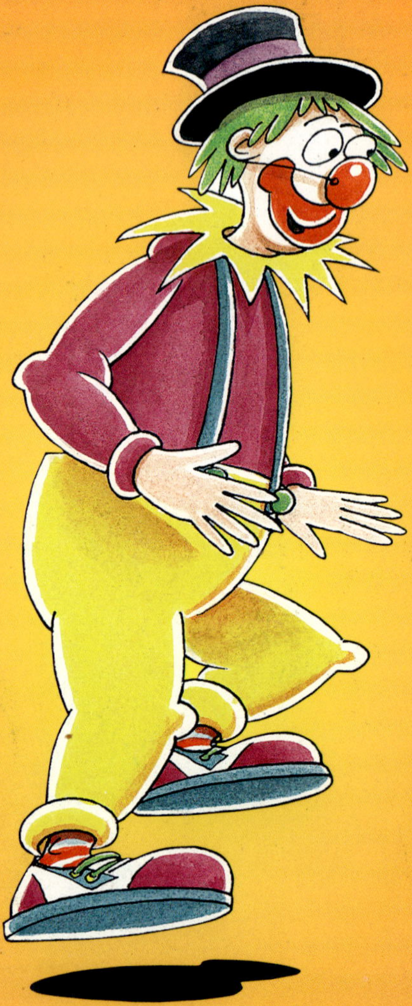

I am hopping.

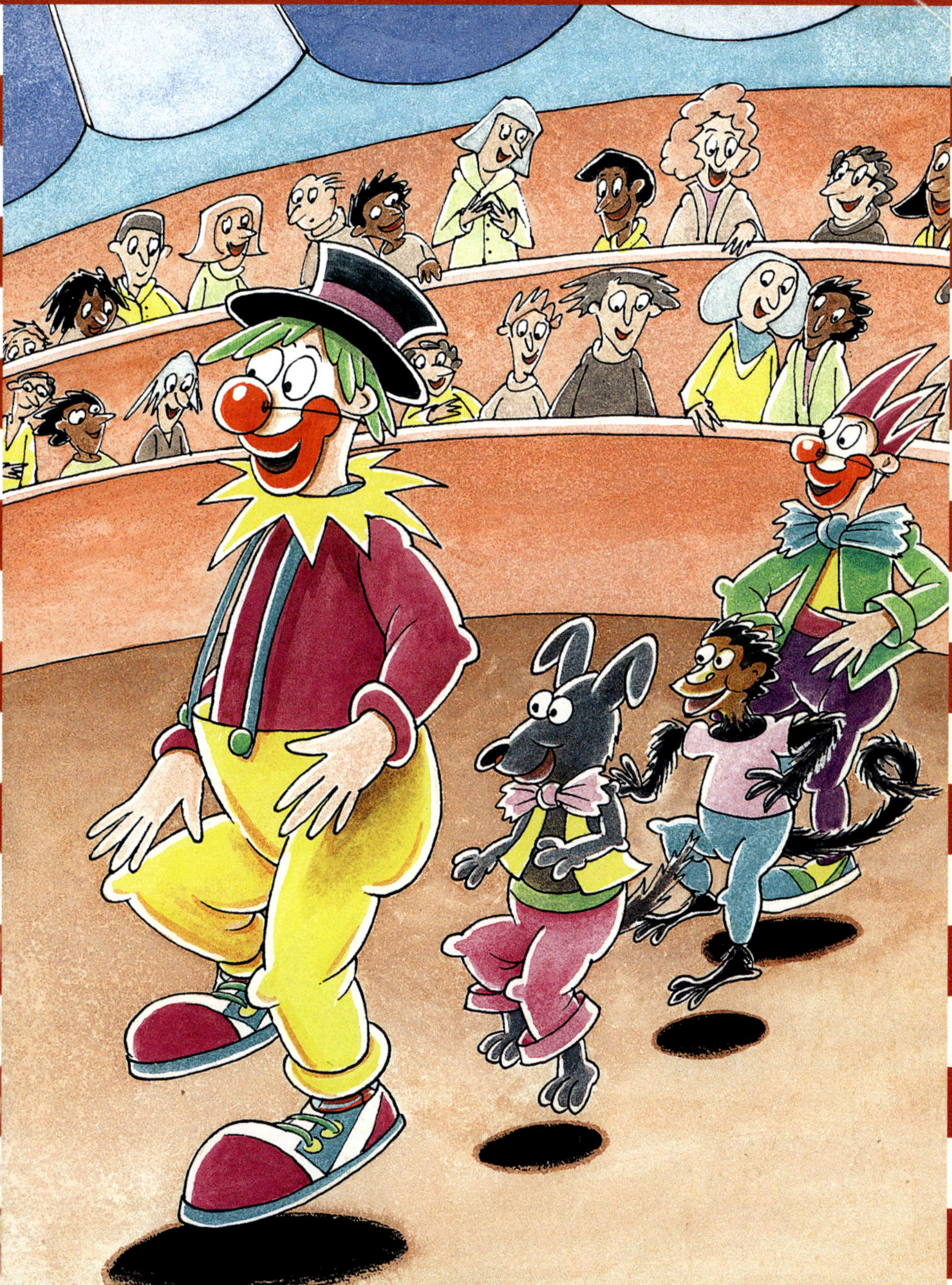

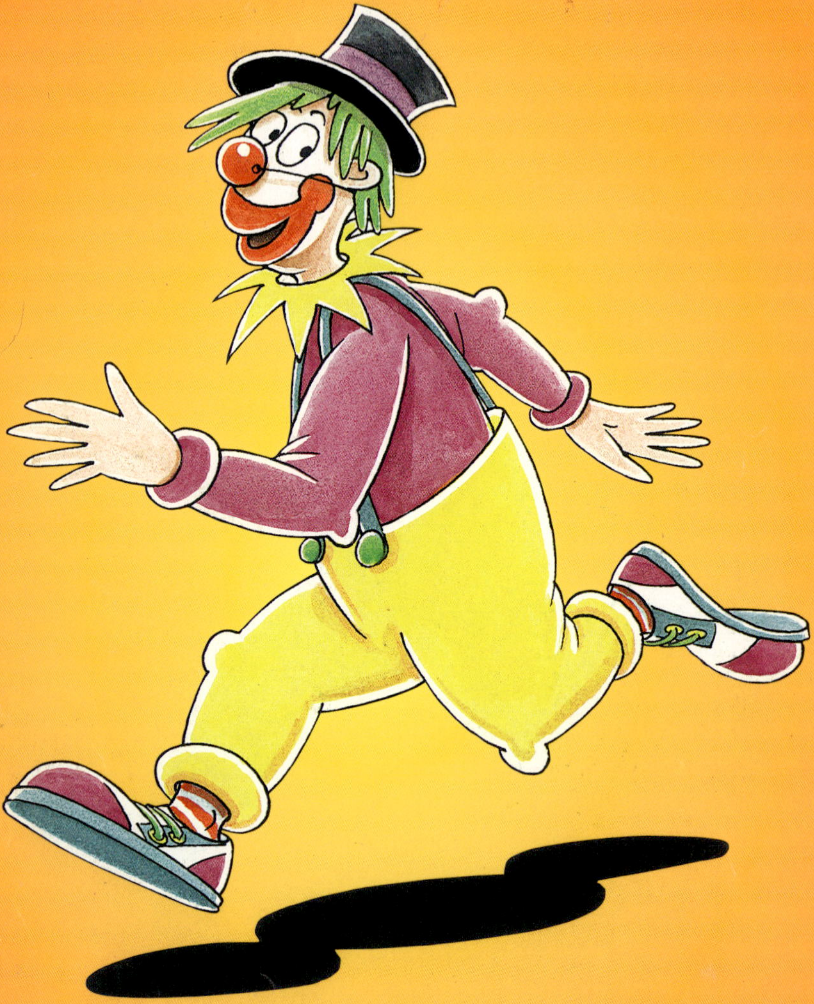

I am running.